How a Tadpole Grows Into a Frog

Written by
David Stewart

Illustrated by
Carolyn Franklin

croak

croak!

Hold the page
up to the light
and see if you
can see the
frog's skeleton.

children's press®
An Imprint of Scholastic Inc.
NEW YORK • TORONTO • LONDON • AUCKLAND • SYDNEY
MEXICO CITY • NEW DELHI • HONG KONG
DANBURY, CONNECTICUT

ISBN-13: 978-0-531-20443-6 (lib. bdg.)   978-0-531-20454-2 (pbk.)
ISBN-10: 0-531-20443-X (lib. bdg.)   0-531-20454-5 (pbk.)

Published in 2008 in the United States
by Children's Press, an imprint of Scholastic Inc.,
557 Broadway, New York, NY 10012.

SCHOLASTIC and associated logos are trademarks and/or
registered trademarks of Scholastic Inc.

Copyright © 2008 by
The Salariya Book Company Ltd
25 Marlborough Place, Brighton BN1 1UB, England.
All rights reserved.

A CIP catalog record for this book is available
from the Library of Congress.

Author: **David Stewart** has written many nonfiction books for children on historical topics, including *You Wouldn't Want to be an Egyptian Mummy!* and *You Wouldn't Want to Sail on the Titanic!* He lives in Brighton, England, with his wife and son.

Artist: **Carolyn Franklin** is a graduate of Brighton College of Art, England, specializing in design and illustration. She has worked in animation, advertising, and children's fiction and nonfiction. She has a special interest in natural history and has written many books on the subject, including *Life in the Wetlands* in the WHAT ON EARTH? series and *Egg to Owl* in the CYCLES OF LIFE series.

Consultant: **Monica Hughes** is an experienced Educational Advisor and author of more than one hundred books for young children. She has been headteacher of a primary school, primary advisory teacher and senior lecturer in early childhood education.

Printed and bound in China.
Printed on paper from sustainable sources.

Contents

What Is a Frog?

A frog begins life as an egg. A tadpole hatches from the egg. The tadpole slowly grows into a small frog called a froglet, and then it becomes an adult frog.

five toes

splash

Frogs have four toes on
their front feet and five
toes on their back feet.

splash

splash

four toes

Where Do Frogs Live?

Frogs live some of the time in ponds and streams. They also live on land, in grassy damp areas near water. Animals that live both in water and on land are called amphibians.

dragonfly

water lily

cattails

There are a lot of frogs in this pond. One frog is sitting on a lily pad and another frog is jumping.

croak
croak

lily pad

What Sounds Do Frogs Make?

In the spring, frogs look for a partner. The male frog calls to a female frog. He makes the sides of his throat swell up and croaks very loudly so that she will notice him.

croak
croak
croak

grunt

chirp
chirp
chirp

The female frog then answers
him in grunts and chirps.

Do Frogs Lay Eggs?

When the male has found a female, the two frogs mate. The female frog lays about three thousand eggs. Then the male frog fertilizes the eggs and they begin to grow.

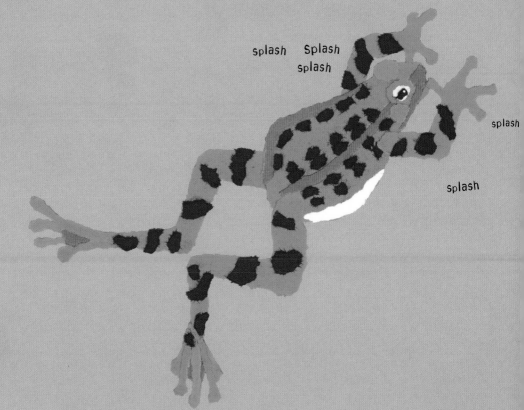

splash Splash
splash
splash
splash

As the eggs start to grow, they stick together. The eggs are now called frog spawn.

frog spawn

What Are Tadpoles?

Each egg grows inside a tiny ball of jelly. See how the eggs start to change shape. As they grow larger, they grow a head and a tail.

egg

head

tail

After a few days, tadpoles hatch. Tadpoles live underwater and breathe through their gills.

gills

tadpole

The **gills** are the big feathery flaps on either side of the tadpole's head.

13

What Do Tadpoles Eat?

At first tadpoles eat only tiny water plants. As they get bigger, they start to eat small animals such as water fleas and pond worms.

munch
munch

small
back
legs

As it grows bigger and bigger, the tadpole starts to grow back legs.

What Happens to the Tadpole's Tail?

front legs

The tadpole's tail gets smaller and smaller. Soon it starts to grow two front legs. It is now starting to look like a frog.

Tadpoles use their long back legs for swimming. Can you see the thin pieces of skin between the toes? This is called **webbing.**

Webbed feet help the tadpole push itself through the water faster. This means it can swim quickly to catch food or get away from danger.

splash
splash

webbed
feet

Can the Froglets Breathe Air?

The tadpoles have now grown into young frogs called froglets. The froglets can put their heads out of the water and breathe air.

croak
croak

See how small the tail is now!

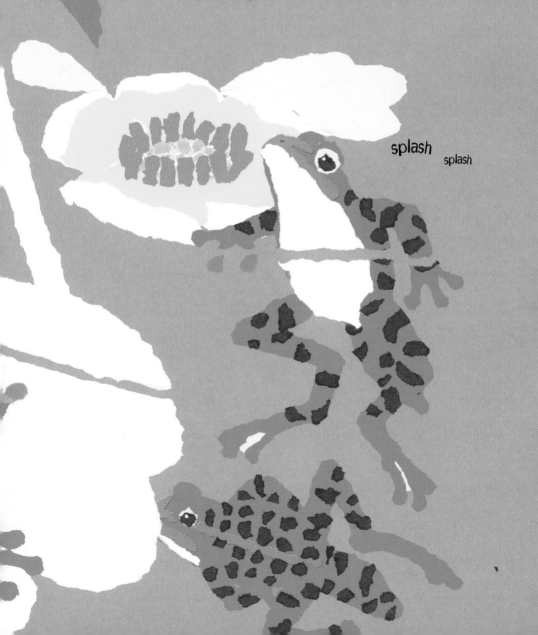

damselfly

These froglets will soon leave the water and live on land. They have stopped using their gills and started to use their **lungs** to breathe.

splash splash

19

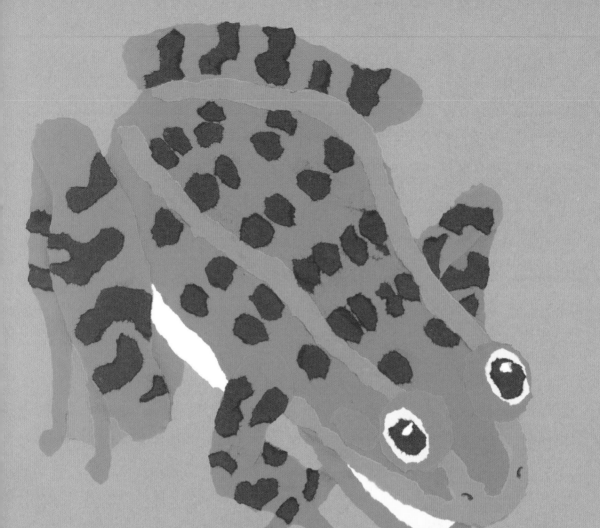

What Do Froglets Eat?

The froglets climb out of the water to look for food. They like to eat slugs and snails.

snail

insect

gulp

gulp

Frogs and froglets have long,
sticky tongues that are good
for catching insects.

slug

What Dangers Do Froglets Face?

Cats like to chase froglets. Many other creatures like to eat them. The froglets must quickly jump away and try to hide from danger.

croak
croak

croak
croak

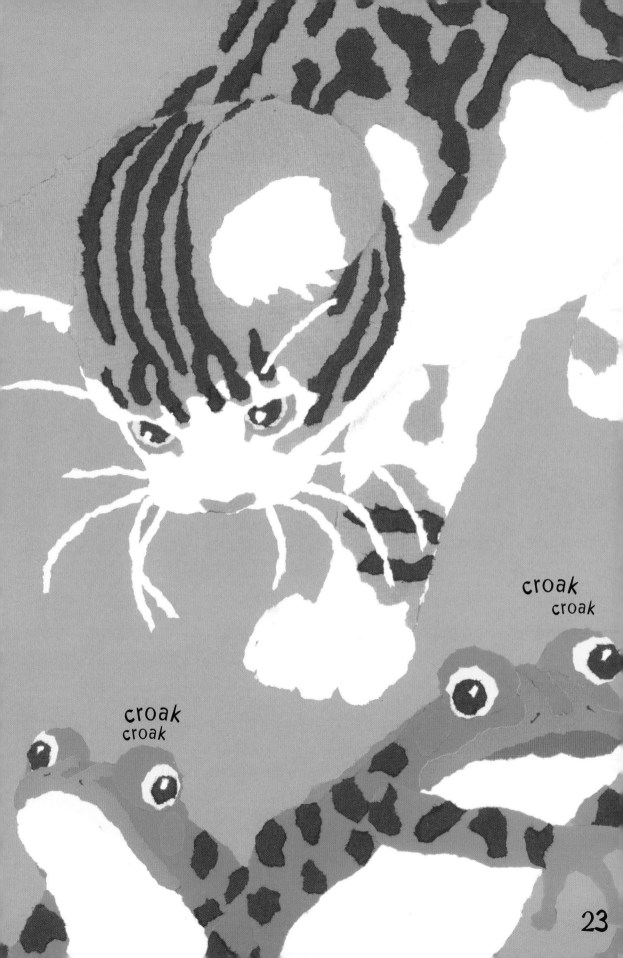

23

How Long Does It Take for a Froglet to Grow Into a Frog?

Slowly the froglets grow into adult frogs. After three years, the adult male frog will look for a mate. Then the female frog will lay eggs and the cycle of life will begin again.

croak
croak

Things to Do

How to Look Inside a Pond

You will need:

One large clear plastic bottle

Scissors

Transparent tape

Clear plastic wrap

1 Ask an adult to cut off the top and bottom of the bottle.

2 Carefully tape a piece of plastic wrap to the base of the bottle.

3 Put the covered end of the bottle just below the surface of the pond. Look down into the other end.

How does it work?

It is usually very difficult to see into a pond because the top of the water is very shiny and reflects light. By using this tube to look through the water, you can look straight down and see what is underneath the surface.

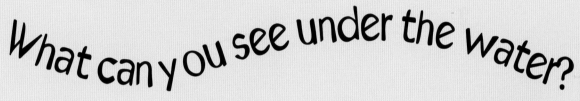

What can you see under the water?

Where Do Frogs Go in the Winter?

When it starts to get cold, adult frogs hibernate. They hide under a pile of mud and leaves at the bottom of the pond and go to sleep.

A frog will hibernate for about 4 months.

Keep a Frog Diary

My Frog Diary

Date: March 6th

I saw lots of frog spawn.

Date: March 13th

In early spring, visit your local pond every few days to look out for frog spawn. A week later, look for tadpoles. Each time you visit the pond, write down the date and what you have seen.

28

A Frog's Year*

Winter

The frog hibernates. It wakes up for a short while, then goes back to sleep.

Winter/Spring

The frog has woken up. It goes to find a mate.

Spring

The female frog lays her eggs. Tadpoles start to hatch.

Spring

More and more tadpoles hatch. The tadpoles feed and grow bigger.

Spring

Tadpoles grow back legs. Their tails get smaller. Then they grow front legs.

Summer

Some of the tiny froglets leave the pond.

Summer

The other froglets leave the pond.

Summer

The adult frog lives in long grass.

Fall

Froglets eat lots of food. Their body stores the food and they grow fat.

Fall

As it gets colder, the frog finds a place to hibernate.

Fall

Some of the young frogs are still looking for food.

Winter

Most of the frogs are hibernating. Frogs often wake up for a short time to feed.

29

* These are approximate times. Each frog lives in a different habitat and has its own timescale.

How a Frog Grows

Egg

One week

Seven weeks

Nine weeks

Twelve weeks

Fourteen weeks

Words to Remember

Adult Grown-up

Amphibians Animals that spend some time in the water and some time on land. They begin their lives in water.

Froglet A young frog.

Fertilization When female and male reproductive cells join together.

Frog spawn The sticky mass of eggs that floats on the surface of the water. Tadpoles hatch from frogspawn.

Gills These are needed by animals to breathe underwater. They are on either side of a tadpole's head. As froglets grow, they lose their gills and grow lungs.

30

Twenty weeks

Fully grown

Hibernate To go to sleep during the winter.

Lungs These are needed by animals to breathe air. They are inside the body.

Male reproductive cell The cell from the male that joins the egg from the female to produce a baby.

Tadpole A frog when it is in the first stage of its life cycle.

Webbed feet Feet with stretched skin between the toes. Webbed feet help frogs to swim.

Index